GREAT BUILDINGS

THE HOUSES OF PARLIAMENT

Nigel Smith

WAYLAND

GREAT BUILDINGS

THE COLOSSEUM
HE EMPIRE STATE BUILDING
THE GREAT PYRAMID
HE HOUSES OF PARLIAMENT
THE PARTHENON
THE TAJ MAHAL

Produced for Wayland Publishers Limited by
The Creative Publishing Company Limited
Unit 3, 37 Watling Street, Leintwardine
Shropshire SY7 OLW, England

Series designers: Ian Winton and Sally Boothroyd
Book designer: Sally Boothroyd
Series editor: Alex Woolf
Book editor: Sabrina Crewe
Illustrations: Mike White
Map and plan: Peter Bull

First published in 1997 by
Wayland Publishers Limited
61 Western Road, Hove
East Sussex BN3 1JD, England

Find Wayland on the internet at http://www.wayland.co.uk

British Library Cataloguing in Publication Data
Smith, Nigel, 1947-
Houses of Parliament. - (Great buildings)
1.Great Britain. Parliament - History - Juvenile literature
2.Palace of Westminster - Juvenile literature 3.Public buildings - England - London - Design and construction - Juvenile literature
I.Title II.Smith, Mike
725.1'1'0942132

ISBN 0 7502 1992 0

Printed and bound in Italy by G. Canale & C.S.p.A., Turin

CONTENTS

IN THE THIRD YEARE OF FREEDOME BY GODS BLESSING RESTORED 1651

INTRODUCTION

WESTMINSTER IN FLAMES

Huge flames lit up the night sky. It was October 1834, and a fire was raging in the heart of London. The Houses of Parliament were burning. Soldiers struggled to control thousands of onlookers. Small boats jostled each other on the River Thames to get the best view. It was the biggest blaze seen in London since the Great Fire, 168 years earlier.

The Prime Minister, Lord Melbourne, was desperately directing efforts to save the buildings. The fire brigade did all they could, but the flames were too great for their simple pumps. The firemen worked frantically, managing to save the historic Westminster Hall. The rest of the buildings became smouldering ruins.

▲ St. Stephen's Chapel, which had been used as the House of Commons for nearly 300 years, was completely ruined by the fire of 1834.

Among the crowds thronging around Westminster was the architect Charles Barry. He knew that the Houses of Parliament would have to be rebuilt, but he didn't yet know that he would be the man to do it.

'England is the mother of Parliaments.'

John Bright, Member of Parliament, 1865

CHAPTER ONE

THE BEGINNINGS OF PARLIAMENT

▼ The Houses of Parliament are situated by the River Thames in Westminster, an area of London. The 'Houses' are actually parts of one huge building called the Palace of Westminster.

The United Kingdom of Great Britain and Northern Ireland is very proud of its system of parliamentary government. It is a system that has been adopted by several other countries. To many people, the Houses of Parliament are an impressive reminder of the British system of government. The Houses of Parliament we see today were built after the fire of 1834, but the history of Parliament goes back much further.

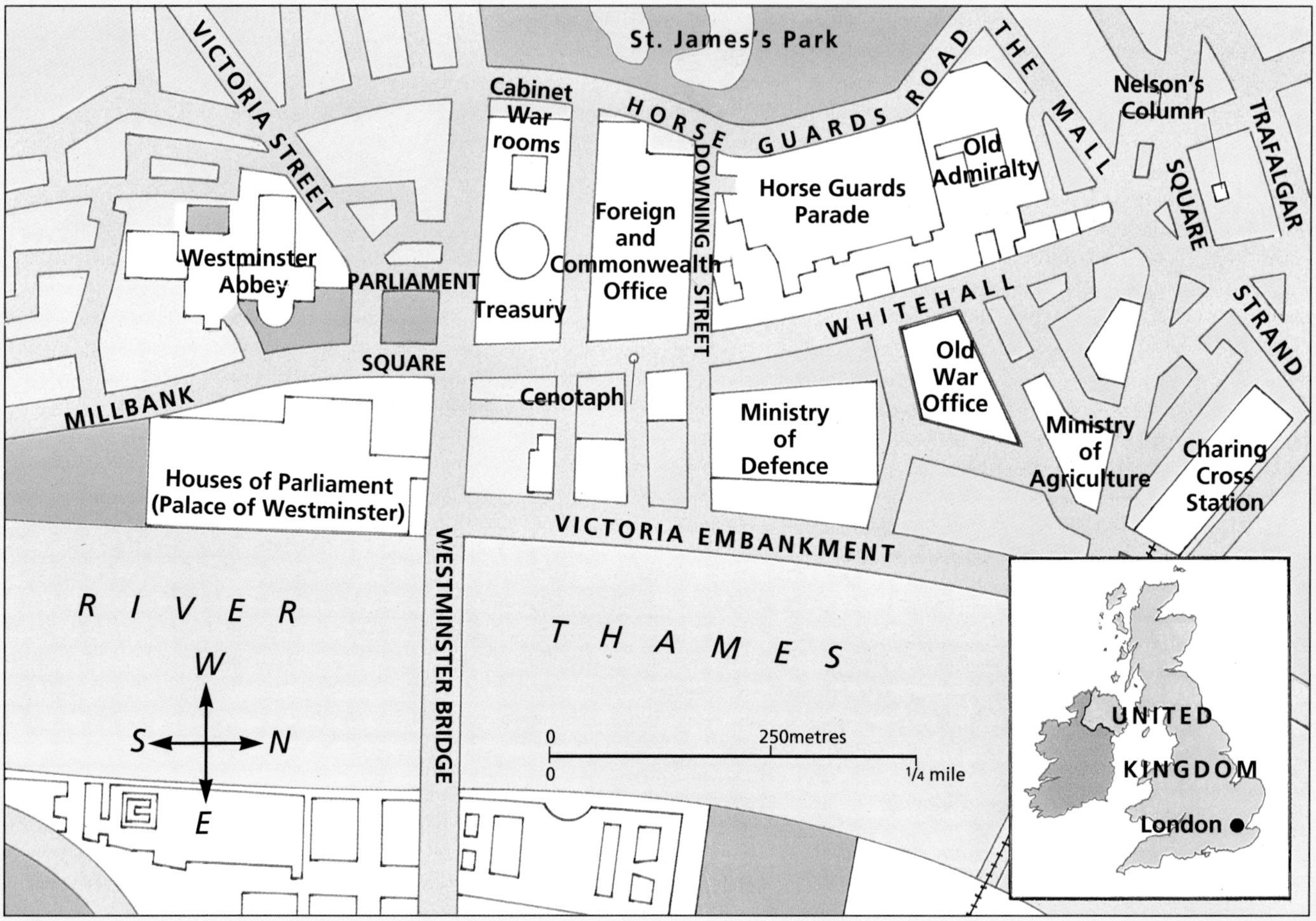

St. James's Park
VICTORIA STREET
HORSE GUARDS ROAD
THE MALL
Cabinet War rooms
Nelson's Column
TRAFALGAR SQUARE
Old Admiralty
Horse Guards Parade
Foreign and Commonwealth Office
DOWNING STREET
Westminster Abbey
PARLIAMENT SQUARE
Treasury
WHITEHALL
STRAND
Cenotaph
Old War Office
MILLBANK
Ministry of Defence
Ministry of Agriculture
Charing Cross Station
Houses of Parliament (Palace of Westminster)
VICTORIA EMBANKMENT
WESTMINSTER BRIDGE
RIVER THAMES
W
S
N
E
0
250metres
0
1/4 mile
UNITED KINGDOM
London

More than twelve hundred years ago, the kings of Anglo-Saxon England used to take advice from leading nobles and churchmen. Their meetings were called the Witenagemot, meaning 'council of the wise'. This was the earliest type of Parliament.

▲ The Witenagemot was the supreme council of an Anglo-Saxon kingdom. This illustration from an Anglo-Saxon manuscript shows a king with his Witenagemot. The Witenagemot advised the king on laws and taxes, and even helped to choose a new king if the succession was in doubt.

In the time of William the Conqueror (1066-1087), the Witenagemot began to be called the Great Council. The members of the Great Council were still leading men, but they had little power. The king gave them land in return for their loyalty, and they were careful not to disagree with him.

During the Middle Ages the king was very much in charge of the country. He chose when the Great Council would meet. By the early fourteenth century, the Great Council had been given the name of Parliament. The name comes from a Latin word meaning discussion. Gradually the meetings grew larger; not only did the rich and powerful lords attend, but also some less important citizens, such as merchants and knights.

The Chancellors Seat

Before long, elections were held to choose Members of Parliament (MPs), although only rich men were allowed to vote. The elected Members of Parliament began to hold their meetings separately from the lords, and were called the House of Commons. They spent

◀ The House of Lords in the time of Queen Elizabeth I (1558-1603). The Members of the House of Commons can be seen in the foreground. By the end of Queen Elizabeth's reign, the House of Commons had 462 members. The Commons still attend the House of Lords every year when the monarch opens Parliament.

IN·THE·THIRD·YEARE·OF·FREEDOME·BY·GODS·BLESSING·RESTORED·1651

◀ This Great Seal of England shows the House of Commons in 1651. The seal was used during the Commonwealth (1653-1660), when there was no monarch ruling Britain. In 1660 the monarchy was restored, but monarchs never again had as much power as in the past.

their time discussing new laws to put forward to the king. The dukes, earls and barons (collectively known as lords, or peers) continued to meet with the king. They called themselves the House of Lords.

The Speaker of the House

One of the most important members of the House of Commons is the Speaker of the House. This brass effigy shows a Speaker from the fifteenth century called William Catesby. The original job of the Speaker was to report the views of the Commons' members to the king, a difficult and even dangerous job. The king often disliked the Commons' decisions, but Speakers insisted that MPs should be free to say whatever they liked, without fear. Today, this freedom of speech is a very important part of Parliament. The Speaker still presides over the meetings, calling the other Members to speak and making sure that they obey the rules.

CHAPTER TWO

THE PALACE OF WESTMINSTER

During the reign of King Cnut (1016-1035) a royal palace and monastery were built at Westminster, a few kilometres west of the City of London. (The Anglo-Saxon word 'minster' means monastery.) Some years later, King Edward the Confessor (1042-1066) built a proper royal palace at Westminster. Edward also replaced the monastery with the much larger Abbey of St. Peter. When Edward died he was buried in the Abbey, later known as Westminster Abbey.

The Great Roof

The roof added to Westminster Hall between 1394 and 1399 is still the largest of its type in the world. It was built by a carpenter called Hugh Herland, seen inspecting the work with Richard II in this 1924 painting. The existing roof was taken down, and in its place great wooden beams were used to create splendid arches. The only equipment employed for this enormous task was a system of ropes and pulleys, pulled by men and horses. The roof holds itself together by the tension created from the beams pressing against each other.

A View of the Inside of Westminster Hall
This was formerly the chief Palace of the Kings of England, but none of them have resided in it since Henry 8 when great part of it was burnt. This large Hall is 300 foot long & 100 wide, it has the finest Roof of its Kind of any in Christendom, it is made of Irish Oak, buttressed artfully at Top, without any Pillars to support it. On the left hand as you enter, there is a pair of Stairs leading to the Exchequer, where all the publick Mony of the Nation is received and paid out. The right hand Stairs conducts from the Hall to the Court where the Barons of the Exchequer sit on all causes relating to the Revenue, and likewise to Equity. Near y middle of the Hall on the Right is the Common Pleas between Man & Man. And at the upper End are kept the Courts of Chancery for Causes of Equity, and the Court of Kings Bench for Criminal Causes and pleas of the Crown. It is in this Hall the Kings and Queens of England feast the Nobility and Gentry at their Coronation. In the upper Apartments is the House of Commons, which was formerly a Chapple belonging to the Palace, and a little beyond that, is the Room where the House of Lords sit.
g

▲ A view of Westminster Hall in the eighteenth century.

For nearly five hundred years Westminster was the main royal palace. William II (1087-1100), made an important addition to the Palace that is still in use today. A new hall was built, three times as long and more than twice as wide as the old Palace. When completed in 1099, Westminster Hall was probably the largest hall in Europe.

Three hundred years later, in the time of King Richard II (1377-1399), Westminster Hall was rebuilt. The walls were made higher and a huge new roof was added. Although other changes have been made since 1399, Westminster Hall, with its great roof, looks much as it did six hundred years ago. It is the oldest remaining part of the original palace, and is now part of the new Palace of Westminster, which these days is more often called the Houses of Parliament.

▼ This seventeenth-century picture gives a wonderful view of the buildings at Westminster. St. Stephen's Chapel on the left had become Parliament House, where the House of Commons met. The huge roof of Westminster Hall can be seen in the middle. It appears much smaller today, since the new Houses of Parliament have been built around it. Westminster Abbey is on the right.

Henry VIII (1509-1547) was the last king to live at Westminster Palace. Henry was a keen sportsman and liked to play tennis inside Westminster Hall. In the 1920s some of his tennis balls were found, still stuck in the roof beams. By Henry's time, Westminster Hall was used mainly as a law court, and many famous trials took place there. After 1529, Henry built a new palace at Whitehall, and the Palace of Westminster became used only for the business of law and government. There were plenty of empty rooms that could be used by Members of Parliament.

From 1352, the House of Commons had met nearby in the Chapter House of Westminster Abbey. In 1547 the House of Commons settled into the Old Palace chapel, St. Stephen's. It was their permanent home until 1834.

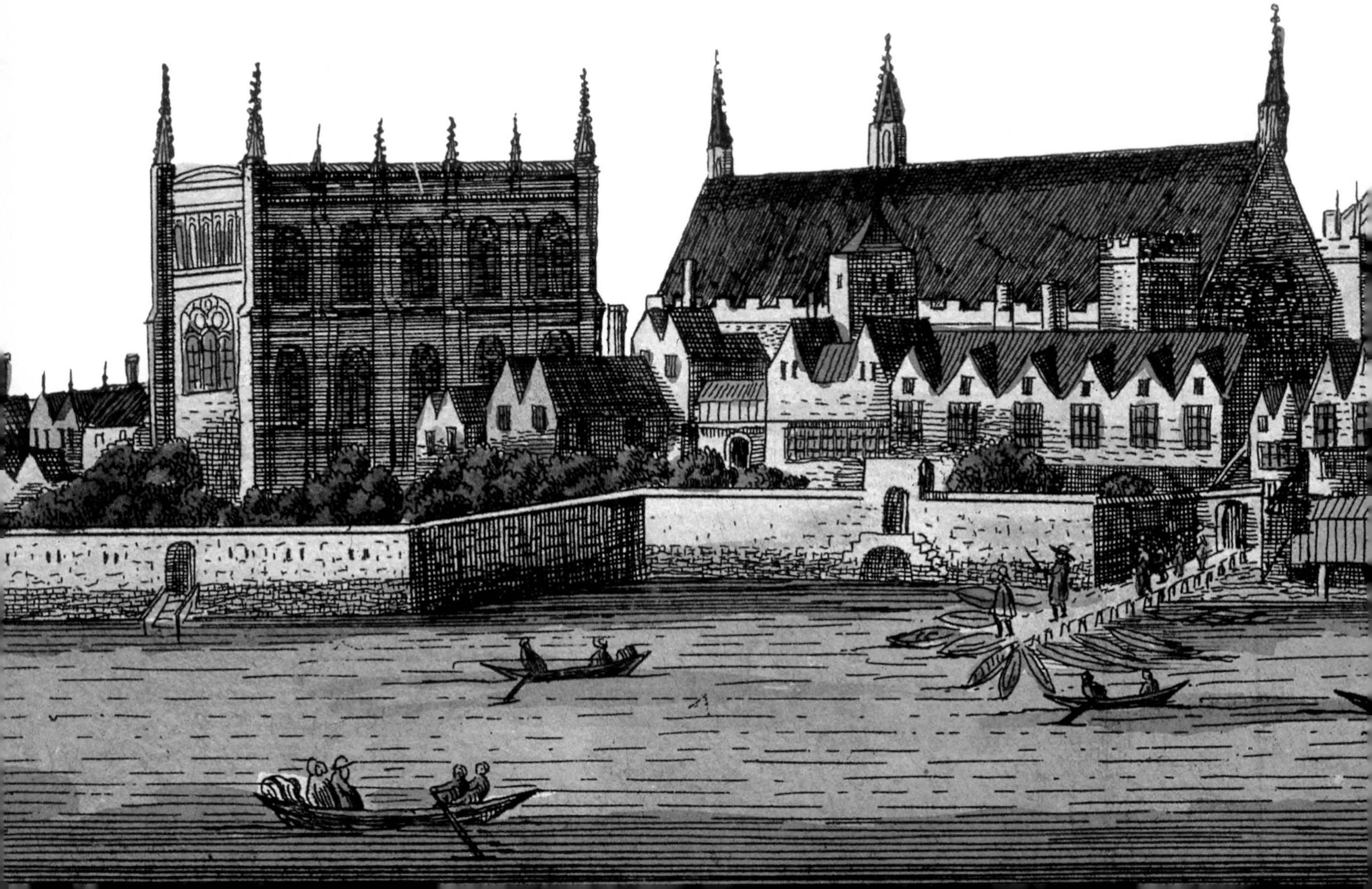

The chapel became known as Parliament House. The altar was replaced by the Speaker's chair, and the chapel stalls were used as seats for the Members of Parliament. Because worshippers had sat facing each other, the MPs also sat facing one another. Today, the modern House of Commons is arranged in the same way.

▲ The House of Commons in St. Stephen's Chapel, where it met for nearly three hundred years. This nineteenth-century illustration was drawn by Thomas Rowlandson and Auguste Charles Pugin. Pugin was the father of Augustus Welby Pugin, the man who was responsible for decorating the new Houses of Parliament some years later.

'Remember,
remember,
the fifth of
November,
Gunpowder
treason and plot.
I see no reason
why gunpowder
treason
Should ever be
forgot.'

A traditional rhyme

◀ The Gunpowder Plot is remembered every year on 5 November, when bonfires are lit and fireworks explode all over Britain.

CHAPTER THREE

KINGS AND PARLIAMENT

In 1605, an attempt was made to blow up Parliament. For many years, Roman Catholics had been persecuted for refusing to recognize the monarch as head of the Christian Church. Finally, a group of angry Catholics hatched a plot to kill King James I. They planned to blow up the House of Lords when the king was present during the opening of Parliament. The plotters hid 36 barrels of gunpowder underneath the House before the night of 5 November. But the plot was discovered, and the conspirators executed.

Searching the Vaults
Every year since the Gunpowder Plot, the Yeomen of the Guard search the vaults under the Houses of Parliament before the monarch arrives for the State Opening. The search is no longer done as a safety precaution. Nowadays security at the Palace of Westminster is a much more complicated and serious business. Searching the vaults has become instead one of several traditional ceremonies that take place in and around the Houses of Parliament.

▼ Charles I's attempt to arrest his opponents in the House of Commons was a failure. The five MPs managed to elude his soldiers by climbing through a window.

Many arguments took place between kings and Parliament. The main argument was over who should have the most power. These disagreements reached boiling point in the time of King Charles I (1625-1649). He believed kings were chosen by God, and that Parliament should always agree with their monarch. Members of Parliament believed that the king should take their advice.

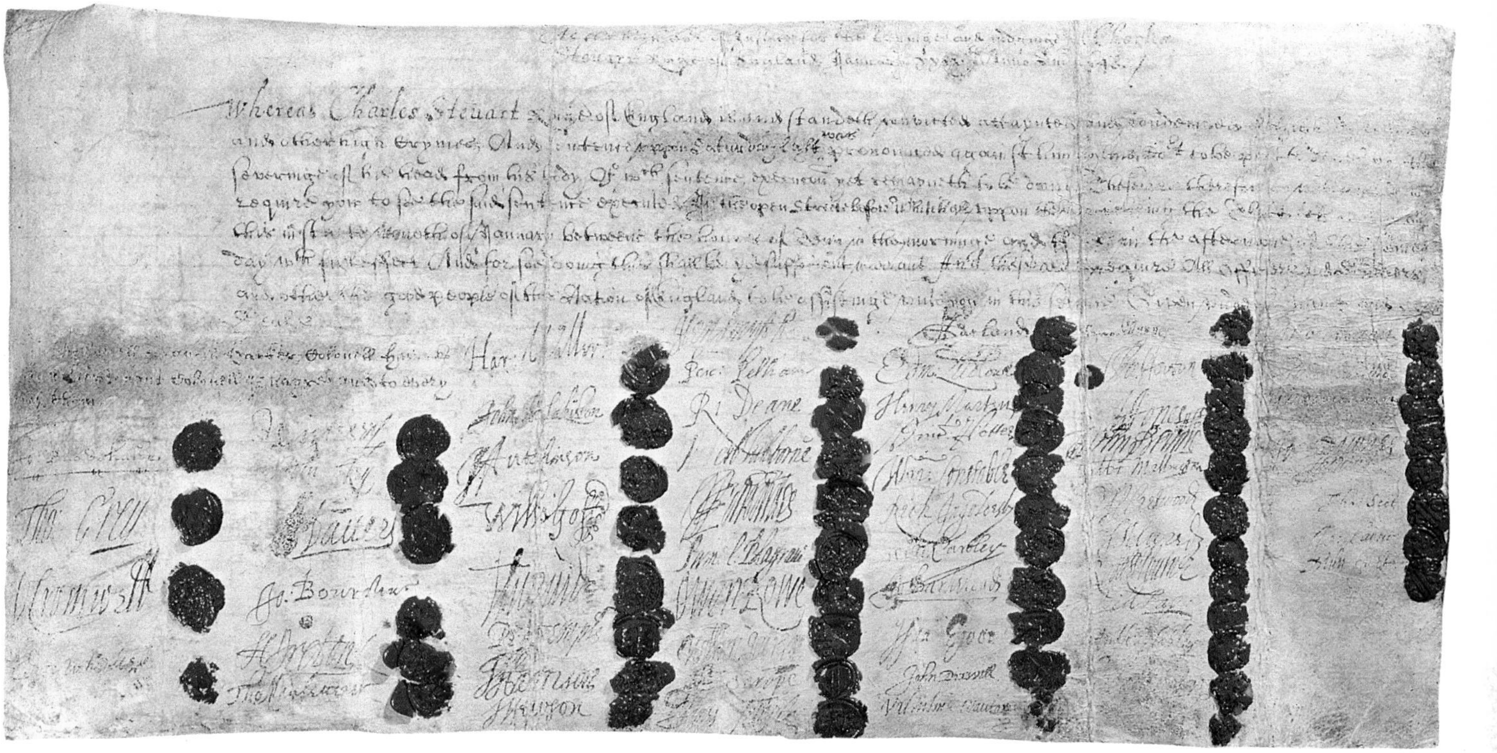

▲ In 1649, Charles I, named 'a tyrant, traitor and murderer', was found guilty of causing a war and harming his own subjects. This death warrant ordered his execution, and he was beheaded on 30 January 1649.

On several occasions Parliament refused to give the king money that he asked for. In 1642 Charles was so angry that he entered the House of Commons with 300 soldiers. There he tried to arrest five MPs, but they escaped into a boat on the River Thames.

The king's action was the last straw. The country was split and a civil war broke out between king and Parliament. After many battles, the king was beaten. In 1646 he became Parliament's prisoner.

Three years later King Charles was put on trial in Westminster Hall. He said that because he was the king they had no right to judge him. However, he was sentenced to death, and executed outside his own palace at Whitehall. For eleven years Britain had no monarch. Later the monarchy was restored and Charles' son became the new king. Gradually, Parliament became more powerful, and never again did a monarch ignore the views of Parliament.

CHAPTER FOUR

THE PLAN FOR THE NEW BUILDING

▼ The old Palace of Westminster was a dreadful fire hazard. By the nineteenth century it had become a jumble of shops, public houses, offices, committee rooms and lodging-houses for MPs. All the time there were crowds of people bustling about. There were no fire precautions, and warnings that a fire would spread quickly were ignored.

The fire of 1834 was started by a workman who had been burning old wooden tally sticks in a stove. Eager to get the job done, he piled on too many and the fire quickly got out of control.

Fire-fighting equipment was primitive. Firemen sprayed water from the nearby River Thames on to the roof of Westminster Hall and saved it from burning down. But the rest of the Palace of Westminster was badly damaged. Many important and historic documents were lost in the flames.

◀ According to eyewitnesses, flames were leaping ten metres above the roof of the House of Lords only fifteen minutes after the fire started.

'The old walls stood triumphantly midst the scene of ruin while brick walls and framed sashes, slate roofs etc. fell faster than a pack of cards.'

Augustus Pugin, in a letter dated 6 November 1834

Out of the disaster came a wonderful opportunity. The government announced a competition to design new Houses of Parliament. There was great excitement among architects, and 97 designs were put forward. The winning design was by Charles Barry, who was given the job of designing Britain's most important building.

Sir Charles Barry (1795-1860)
This statue of Charles Barry stands in the Palace of Westminster that he designed. At the age of 15, Barry started work with a firm of architects. When he had saved some money, he travelled all over Europe and as far as Egypt to study buildings. Barry used Italian and Egyptian styles in some of the buildings that he designed. He designed several churches and other major buildings, but the Houses of Parliament were his most important assignment. The long hours of hard work and worry damaged Barry's health, and he died before the Houses of Parliament were completed.

In Barry's plan, the new Houses of Parliament and all their offices would become one huge building. The new building would contain more than 1,100 rooms. Some would be large and grand, such as committee rooms and libraries. Many would be small offices for MPs, peers and their staff. Barry planned a hundred staircases and more than three kilometres of passages.

There were to be no chimneys. All the smoke from fires and stoves would go into great shafts that from the outside looked like elegant turrets. The tallest one, the Central Tower, would stand 91.4 metres high. Other shafts would bring fresh air into every part of the building. This ventilation and heating system would be the most advanced in the world, although it caused great problems when it was first installed.

▼ Barry planned the new Houses of Parliament around eleven courtyards. The courts, as they are called, provide air and light to the rooms inside the building. You can see where some of the courts are in this aerial photograph. You can also see the Central Tower, the tallest of the air shafts, in the middle of the building.

Gothic Architecture

Barry's design was in the Gothic style of architecture, which had been used in the Middle Ages to build cathedrals and churches. Gothic buildings have high arches and towers. The stonework is highly decorated, and statues and stained glass windows are often used. Gothic architecture became popular again in the nineteenth century, partly because of the new Houses of Parliament. The style was used for all kinds of buildings including railway stations, hotels and town halls.

It took Barry six months to draw up the plans. He thought that the whole building could be finished in six years. He was badly mistaken. The new Houses of Parliament took about thirty years to complete.

▼ This is a plan of the main floor of the Palace of Westminster. It shows that the House of Lords and House of Commons are just parts of the whole building.

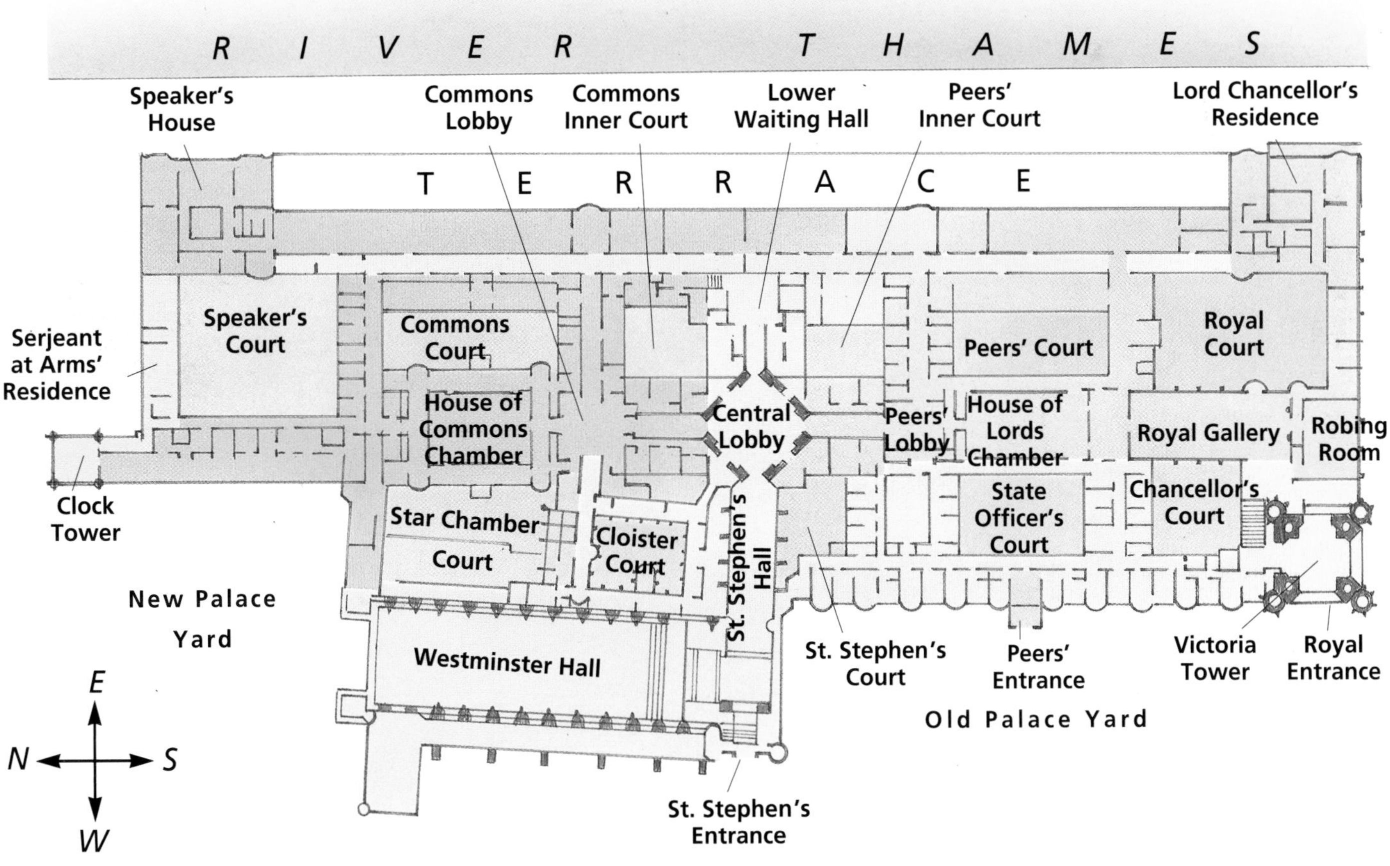
R I V E R T H A M E S
Speaker's House
Commons Lobby
Commons Inner Court
Lower Waiting Hall
Peers' Inner Court
Lord Chancellor's Residence
T E R R A C E
Serjeant at Arms' Residence
Speaker's Court
Commons Court
Peers' Court
Royal Court
House of Commons Chamber
Central Lobby
Peers' Lobby
House of Lords Chamber
Royal Gallery
Robing Room
Clock Tower
Star Chamber Court
Cloister Court
St. Stephen's Hall
State Officer's Court
Chancellor's Court
New Palace Yard
Westminster Hall
St. Stephen's Court
Peers' Entrance
Victoria Tower
Royal Entrance
Old Palace Yard
St. Stephen's Entrance
E
N
S
W

CHAPTER FIVE

BUILDING THE HOUSES OF PARLIAMENT

For nearly six years, hundreds of men worked to get the ground ready to start construction. They had to clear away the rubble of the ruined buildings. It was not a good site for a large building. The ground was marshy, and there were times when it became flooded by the River Thames.

The new building was much larger than the old ones and needed good foundations. After a long struggle, the area was drained, and huge concrete foundations were laid. In places they are 3.6 metres thick. The Houses of Parliament are actually built on a kind of giant raft resting on a lake of mud.

◀ Limestone was very good for carving decoration around windows, doorways and the many turrets. This was an important part of the Gothic design. This huge window carved in limestone was added to Westminster Hall by Barry. It overlooks the statue of Richard I (1189-1199), one of several bronze sculptures that can be seen outside the Houses of Parliament.

On 27 April 1840 the building work was ready to start. Sarah Barry, the architect's wife, laid the first stone. Between 1,200 and 1,400 men were employed to work on the site. About 200 of them were skilled workers, such as stonemasons, but most were labourers. Many came from Ireland, where poverty and the terrible potato famine in the 1840s had driven them to England in search of work. These workmen lived in a huge camp of temporary huts next to the site.

Newly built canals meant that it was possible to transport stone, sand and timber quite easily from anywhere in England. After a tour of Britain's stone quarries, Barry and his master stonemason had chosen limestone from Derbyshire and Yorkshire for the new Parliament building. A constant stream of boats transported the stone and other building materials along canals into the River Thames and to a special dock at Westminster.

▼ Huge towers of wooden scaffolding rose upwards as the building work began. Some of the scaffolding reached a height of over 90 metres. It was the highest that had ever been used.

1. Hoist
2. Roof plates
3. Scaffolding
4. Tramway
5. Steam engine
6. Limestone

◀ Over a thousand men worked on the site of the new Houses of Parliament. Even though the latest materials and construction methods were used, it took many years to complete the vast building.

Great architecture is closely linked to engineering. The Industrial Revolution brought with it new methods of building, with cast-iron replacing wood for the framework of buildings. Barry used cast-iron girders and struts to support roofs and to strengthen the high walls. Stone was put around them so that the iron could not be seen. Although cast-iron had been used before, it was the first time this new method of construction had ben used on such an important building.

The Industrial Revolution
Britain was the first industrialized nation. After 1750 factories began to mass produce goods, including parts for buildings, that until then had been made by hand. For the first time steam engines drove machinery. The population grew quickly, and people moved from the country to live in large industrial cities and towns. Engineers built canals and railways linking up every part of the country. Britain became known as 'the workshop of the world'.

Tramways were used to carry materials back and forth. Steam engines drove the hoists that hauled up timbers and heavy stone building blocks. In this way, blocks of stone weighing as much as five tonnes were raised and put in place without any damage. This was very important for the many pieces of carved stonework.

▶ The new Houses of Parliament look rather like the great buildings of the Middle Ages, but Barry used the very latest technology. New methods of ironmaking had been developed, and Barry was able to cover the roof with iron plates about 5 mm thick, so that it could never catch fire. The plates were coated with zinc to stop them rusting.

> 'Every inch of the great building's surface, inside and out, was designed by one man: every panel, every wallpaper, every chair sprang from Pugin's brain, and his last days were spent in designing ink-pots and umbrella stands.'
>
> Kenneth Clark, *The Gothic Revival*

While the construction was going on, there was another great mind at work on the Houses of Parliament. Charles Barry's young assistant, Augustus Pugin, was an expert on Gothic architecture. Although Barry had designed the building, Pugin was responsible for how the inside looked when it was finished. It was Pugin who was in charge of woodcarving, stained glass, metalwork and tiles. From huge gates and windows to tiny keys and clocks, Pugin decorated the Houses of Parliament in fine Gothic style.

Augustus Pugin (1812-1852)
Pugin's father, a French architectural draughtsman, taught him how to draw up plans. Before he was 20, Pugin had designed furniture for Windsor Castle. He was very keen on Gothic architecture, and designed many churches and cathedrals. Pugin worked for years on the Houses of Parliament and created a great masterpiece. However, like Barry, he worked so hard that it ruined his health. For a short time, Pugin was committed to Bedlam, a dreadful asylum for the insane. He was then taken home, and suffered several months of pain and mental illness before he died.

◀ The Royal Gallery is one of the the most splendid rooms in the Palace of Westminster. Its main function is as a route for the monarch's procession at the annual State Opening of Parliament. Before the procession, she gets ready in the Robing Room, which is reached through this carved and painted doorway.

▼ Pugin loved to use brass. This detail of the solid brass door that leads from the House of Lords to the Peers' Lobby gives a good idea of the amount of work that went into individual pieces.

Pugin employed some of the most skilled craftsmen and manufacturers that Britain had to offer. Floors were covered with large and richly-patterned tiles made at the huge Minton factory in Stoke-on-Trent. Every piece of metalwork from Hardman and Company in Birmingham was made to fit in with Pugin's grand design. Windows were painted, doors were carved, imposing pieces of furniture were gilded and inlaid. Everything added to the magnificence of the decorations.

> 'The building stands a great fact, and will be calmly judged eventually on its merits and defects by posterity....'
>
> Edward M Barry, son of Charles Barry, 1858

CHAPTER SIX

THE NEW HOUSES OF PARLIAMENT

The peers managed to move into the House of Lords in 1847, and the House of Commons Chamber was first used in 1850. However, when Charles Barry died in 1860, the Houses of Parliament were still unfinished. Barry's son Edward took over as architect, and work continued until 1870.

The most imposing view of the finished building is seen from across the River Thames. The river front stretches nearly 300 metres, with the Lord

Chancellor's Residence at one end and the Speaker's House at the other. Along the first floor overlooking the river are the committee rooms. They are decorated with wood panelling and large paintings of scenes from British history. The committee rooms are used by groups of MPs to study and discuss new laws, or examine the work of the government. There are now more committees than Barry had planned for, and extra rooms have been provided.

Also overlooking the river are the five rooms provided by Barry for the House of Commons library. The library holds more than 150,000 books and 750,000 other documents. Barry would be astonished to see the number of computers now being used in the library that he designed solely for books.

The Ravages of Time

The Houses of Parliament were in flames again during the Second World War. Night after night during 1940 and 1941, German bombers attacked London. On fourteen separate nights, the Palace of Westminster was hit by bombs, causing a huge amount of damage and making necessary major rebuilding. Other damage has been caused by rain and pollution, which wear away the limestone exterior. Worn stonework is constantly being repaired and replaced.

One of London's greatest landmarks is a part of the Palace of Westminster. The Clock Tower houses the huge bell known as 'Big Ben'. Nobody is sure if Big Ben was named after the pot-bellied Benjamin Hall (Commissioner of Works at the Palace of Westminster 1855-58), or a large prizefighter of the time, called Benjamin Caunt. The tower itself is now often called Big Ben, and is visited by millions of tourists every year.

Building the Clock Tower was an enormous job. It is 97 metres high and took 19 years to complete. No one had ever built such a tall clock tower before. This was also the first time that such a large clock had been so accurate. The clock has four faces, each one nearly seven metres across.

On 11 July 1859, the booming chimes of Big Ben were heard for the first time. Now, millions of British people hear Big Ben every day on the radio.

◀ Sometimes discussions in the Houses of Parliament carry on through the night. A light, known as the Ayrton light, shines at the top of the Clock Tower when either House is sitting late.

▶ At the time of its construction, Big Ben was the biggest bell that had ever been made. It weighed over 13 tonnes and had a diameter of 3 metres. The bell arrived at Westminster in great style, pulled on a cart by sixteen horses. However, it cracked before being installed and had to be recast. The bell was finally placed in the tower in October 1858, winched up by teams of men.

Victoria Tower

In 1852 Queen Victoria (1837-1901) rode in her horse-drawn coach under the arch of Victoria Tower, named in her honour. When it was completed in 1860, the Victoria Tower stood 100 metres high and was the tallest square tower in the world. The great weight of the tower had to be supported by a very strong arch. Barry used cast-iron girders to support the arch, and cast-iron columns rising upwards to support the tower. All of Parliament's records are stored in Victoria Tower. Thousands of documents, including many of Britain's most historic papers, are kept on 9 kilometres of shelving. A huge Union Jack flag flies from Victoria Tower whenever Parliament is meeting.

'At twelve we went to see the new House of Lords, which unfortunately is to be opened without the House of Commons, as the lords are so impatient to get into it. The building is indeed magnificent, in Gothic style, very elaborate and gorgeous. Perhaps there is a little too much brass and gold in the decorations, but the whole effect is very dignified and fine.'

Queen Victoria, writing in her journal of 14 April 1847

In February 1847 the new House of Lords Chamber was used for the first time. Everybody was delighted with Pugin's work, and the chamber is generally considered to be his greatest accomplishment. It is quite beautifully decorated, using masses of red and gold.

The ceiling is covered with many ancient and royal emblems. The lower walls are of carved oak panels, with stained glass windows rising above on both sides, set in huge stone arches. At either end of the chamber are three more arches, as large as the windows and filled with magnificent frescoes.

The monarch's throne and its canopy dominate the chamber in their golden splendour. Carving and gilding the spectacular canopy took several years. The panels behind the throne are decorated with the royal coat of arms and the crests of England, Wales, Scotland and Northern Ireland.

▼ The House of Lords library, designed by Barry, opened in 1848. Today it contains more than 120,000 books, many rescued from the fire of 1834.

In front of the throne is a large padded seat called the Woolsack, where the Lord Chancellor sits. He is the Speaker of the House of Lords. The seat is filled with wool as reminder that in the Middle Ages wool was England's most important trade.

▼ The House of Commons Chamber in 1881. Above the Speaker's Chair was the Reporters' Gallery, where journalists could sit and write reports for the newspapers. Above that, behind the white stonework, was the Ladies' Gallery, where visiting women could sit.

The new House of Commons Chamber kept to the old plan of Members facing one another. The Speaker's Chair sat at the end of the chamber. To the right of the Speaker were the Government benches. To his left were the Opposition parties. By tradition, the distance between them was the same as the length of two swords.

When the Commons finally moved in to their new chamber, many of them complained about it. For a start it was too small. By 1850 there were about 600 MPs, and yet the chamber could seat only 437. The high ceiling was also criticized. MPs complained they couldn't hear what was being said, and the ceiling had to be lowered.

◀ This photograph from *The Illustrated London News* shows Prime Minister Winston Churchill standing in the wreckage of the House of Commons, after it was hit by a bomb in 1941.

Although MPs grumbled about their chamber, they became very fond of it over the years. Sadly, the chamber built by Charles Barry was destroyed by a bomb during the Second World War, on the night of 10 May 1941. The work of Parliament went on, and for a time the House of Commons met in the House of Lords Chamber. The Commons Chamber had to be completely rebuilt. It is the same size as the old one, because MPs decided in the end that a small chamber made it easier to debate with one another. Since there are now 651 MPs, it sometimes gets very crowded.

CHAPTER SEVEN

INSIDE WESTMINSTER

Britain is a parliamentary democracy. In a democracy, people can vote in elections to choose who makes the laws and runs the country. This is something British people now take for granted, but people in Britain had to struggle hard for the right to vote. It has only been since the twentieth century that most adult men and women have been allowed to do so.

While the new Houses of Parliament were being built, working men began to demand the right to vote. Gradually, Members of Parliament came round to the idea that not only the rich landowners should have a choice in who governed the country. However it was not until after the First World War (1914-1918) that everyone was able to vote for their MP.

REFORM

▼ Between 1838 and 1850 the Chartists campaigned for, among other things, the vote for working men. The Chartists believed that every man should have a say in the government of the country. Three times they took huge petitions to the Houses of Parliament. A large procession accompanied their second petition in 1842, but Parliament rejected their demands.

The cry 'Votes for Women' was first heard in the 1890s. Most people thought it was a crazy idea. During the early 1900s the cry became loud and unstoppable. It wasn't fair, women said, that only men chose the government and became Members of Parliament.

Many women became Suffragettes. The Suffragettes organized a campaign to persuade the government to give women the vote. They were refused many times. The Suffragettes became very determined, chaining themselves to railings, smashing windows and digging up golf courses. After the First World War, when women had worked so hard for victory, they finally gained the right to vote.

▲ In 1909, Suffragettes managed to get into the House of Commons and chain themselves to the grille in one of the galleries. On another occasion they poured flour from a gallery on to the heads of MPs below.

▶ The *Daily Chronicle* of 1910 reports on one of the many incidents of protest in the struggle for women's right to vote.

ARREST OF 117 SUFFRAGISTS

FIVE HOURS' RAID ON THE COMMONS.

PREMIER PASSED UNRECOGNISED.

BLACK ROD'S WINDOWS SMASHED.

One hundred and seventeen arrests were made as a result of yesterday's suffragist raid on the House of Commons. This number constitutes a record in the annals of the Women's Social and Political Union. None ... was taken cap-

Parliament today represents all people, and both men and women over the age of 18 can vote. Britain is divided into 651 areas called constituencies. Each constituency has an MP who has been chosen by the people living in the area. MPs from different political parties have different ideas about how the country should be run, and so when people vote in elections, they choose the person whose ideas are closest to their own. The chosen MPs are then supposed to represent the views of the people who voted for them.

MPs represent their constituents in the House of Commons, where laws are made and decisions are taken about governing Britain. The political party with the most MPs forms the government, and the leader of the government is called the Prime Minister. Even though a particular party is in charge of running the country, MPs from all political parties have an equal vote in the House of Commons.

◀ Everybody has the right to come to the Houses of Parliament and ask to see their MP. Members of the public wait in the Central Lobby, under the high vaulted ceiling with its brilliantly-coloured mosaics. When the House of Commons is in session the Central Lobby is very busy, with people passing back and forth through the four great archways leading to other parts of the building.

◀ In 1989, the House of Commons was seen in action on television for the first time. These MPs are sitting beneath remote-control cameras, ready for the first broadcast. Just outside the Commons Chamber is the Members' Lobby, where MPs meet political reporters from newspapers, radio and television. These reporters have come to be known as 'the lobby'. They can mix with MPs, but they must never name anyone who has given them information without that person's permission.

The other part of Parliament is the House of Lords. Although they do not have much power, the Lords still have a say in the making of new laws. They discuss and revise all new proposals from the government before allowing them to become laws. There are well over over 1,000 Members of the House of Lords, although fewer than 300 regularly attend sittings. Most of them are people whose titles have passed to them from their parents. Others have been chosen to be peers because they have made an important contribution to the country. There are also 24 judges and 26 bishops and archbishops who have seats in the House of Lords.

The Palace of Westminster is always full of activity. As well as MPs and peers, there are about 12,000 other people who work there. Since the nineteenth century, the work of Parliament has grown considerably, and there are far more people working in the building than Charles Barry had ever planned for.

Many alterations have been made to the inside of the building. More space has had to be found for thousands of office staff and all their equipment and papers. Windows have been bricked up, and large rooms have been split and converted into small offices. Further changes are always going on to provide other facilities that Barry never dreamed of: computers and television equipment, shops and cafeterias, and even a gymnasium have all been introduced in the last hundred years.

▲ In the summer, MPs and peers entertain their guests on the Terrace overlooking the River Thames. You can see the Speaker's House at the end of the Terrace.

A few people actually live at the Palace of Westminster. The tower called the Speaker's House stands at one end of the river front. The House contains State Apartments, used for official purposes, and a marvellous collection of portraits. The Speaker's residence is on the floor above the State Apartments. The tower at the other end of the river front contains the residence and offices of the Lord Chancellor, who presides over the House of Lords.

Behind the Speaker's House is the Serjeant at Arms' Residence. The Serjeant at Arms is responsible for the smooth running of the whole building. He is in charge of security and decides who gets which office. Traditionally, it is also his job to escort MPs from the House of Commons if they break the rules and the Speaker has ordered them to leave.

Parliament Square, with the Clock Tower rising above it, is always busy with traffic and tourists. Millions of tourists visit London each year and most of them come to see the famous Houses of Parliament. Security is heavy around the building. Police stand guard at all the entrances to guard against terrorist attacks. Anyone without an official pass is thoroughly searched.

▼ The Queen's procession passes through the Royal Gallery as she leaves the Robing Room for the House of Lords at a State Opening of Parliament. She is accompanied by the Prince of Wales.

Every year, usually in October, the Queen rides in her state coach from Buckingham Palace to the Houses of Parliament for the State Opening of Parliament. It is a grand and traditional occasion, and thousands of people gather to watch.

▶ The Serjeant at Arms carries the Mace in front of the Speaker at the State Opening of Parliament. The Mace is an important emblem, symbolizing the power and freedom of the House of Commons.

The Queen arrives at the Palace of Westminster through the arch of Victoria Tower. In the Robing Room she puts on a crimson robe and her great, heavy crown. The Queen walks to the House of Lords and takes her place on the throne. An official called the Gentleman Usher of the Black Rod is sent to ask members of the House of Commons to come and listen to the Queen's speech. Ever since King Charles I tried to arrest MPs in 1641, no monarch has been permitted to enter the House of Commons. Instead, MPs walk to the House of Lords and crowd in the doorway to hear the Gracious Speech, in which the Queen tells of the government's plans for the coming year.

The ceremony has not changed very much in the past 400 years. Ceremony and tradition are an important part of the government of Britain. People often say that they don't think much of politicians, but Parliament still has a great deal of respect. The Houses of Parliament today stand for the political freedom enjoyed by the British people.

TIMELINE

1000-1199

1042-1066
Edward the Confessor builds palace and abbey at Westminster

1099
Westminster Hall completed by William II

1200-1399

1265
Great Parliament meets in Westminster Hall

1332
Commons and Lords hold separate meetings

1400-1599

1512
Henry VIII moves out of Westminster Palace

1547
House of Commons moves to St. Stephen's Chapel

1600-1800

1605
Gunpowder Plot

1642
Charles I attempts to arrest five MPs

1642-48
Civil War between King and Parliament

1649
Charles I tried in Westminster Hall and executed

1653-60
Britain ruled as Commonwealth

1660
Restoration of the monarchy

IN·THE·THIRD·YEARE·OF·FREEDOME·BY·GODS·BLESSING·RESTORED·1651

1800-1849

1834
Fire at Palace of Westminster

1836
Charles Barry chosen as architect of new Houses of Parliament

1840
Building work starts on new Houses of Parliament

1847
House of Lords Chamber completed

1850-1899

1850
House of Commons Chamber completed

1852
Death of Pugin

1859
Big Ben chimes for the first time

1860
Death of Charles Barry

1870
Houses of Parliament completed

1900-1950

1941
Bomb destroys House of Commons Chamber

1950
Rebuilt House of Commons Chamber completed

1951-2000

1974
Terrorist bomb damages Westminster Hall

1978
Radio broadcasting of Parliament started

1989
First televison broadcast from House of Commons

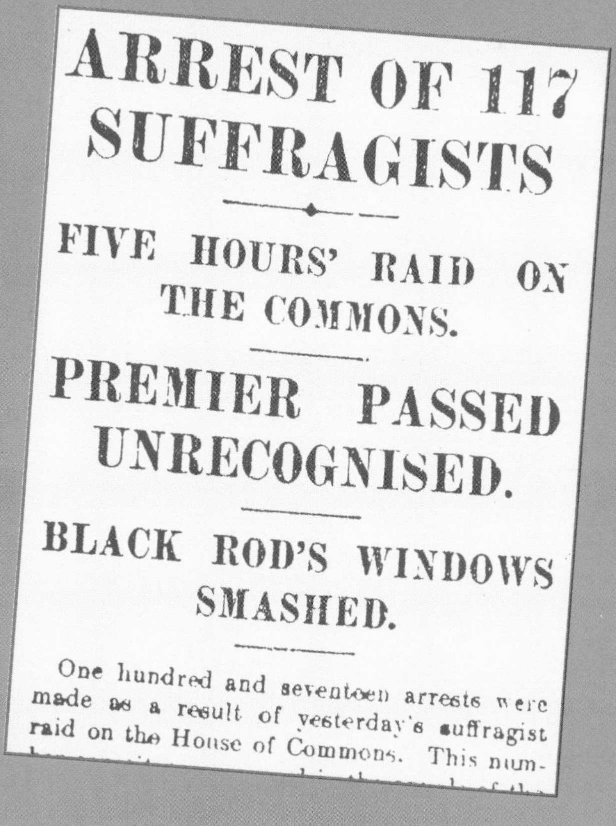
ARREST OF 117 SUFFRAGISTS

FIVE HOURS' RAID ON THE COMMONS.

PREMIER PASSED UNRECOGNISED.

BLACK ROD'S WINDOWS SMASHED.

One hundred and seventeen arrests were made as a result of yesterday's suffragist raid on the House of Commons. This num-

GLOSSARY

Air shaft
A vent which takes air or smoke upwards and out of a building.

Democracy
A system in which people elect a government.

Election
The time when people vote for a person of their choice.

Foundations
The base on which a building is built.

Fresco
A painting on a wall or ceiling.

Great Seal
An engraved piece of metal used to make a mark on important government papers and show that they are genuine. The seal is pressed into wax melted on the document, so that it leaves its image when the wax hardens.

Hoist
A machine that lifts objects off the ground. The hoists used on the Houses of Parliament lifted stonework into place both on the inside and outside of the building.

Monarch
A king or queen. In Britain the monarch is head of the country's government but has no real power.

Opposition
The second largest political party in the House of Commons is the official Opposition and sits opposite the government. MPs belonging to other, smaller parties also sit on the opposition benches.

Peer
Another name for a member of the House of Lords.

Petition
A written request from many people for the government to do a particular thing.

Political party
A group of people with similar ideas as to how the country should be governed.

Tally stick
A notched wooden stick used for keeping records of taxes.

Tradition
Something which has been done for a long time in a certain way.

FURTHER INFORMATION

VISITS

The best person to help you visit the Houses of Parliament is your Member of Parliament. You can write to your MP at the House of Commons, Palace of Westminster, London SW1A 0AA. Members of the public are admitted into the Strangers' Gallery of the House of Commons.

The Jewel Tower, opposite the Houses of Parliament, was built in 1365-66 as part of the old Palace of Westminster. It has a small display about the history of Parliament and is open to the public.

To find out more, you can contact the following information offices:
The House of Lords –
telephone no: (0171) 219 3107
The House of Commons –
telephone no: (0171) 219 4272
The Jewel Tower –
telephone no: (0171) 222 2219

VIDEOS

Westminster Behind Closed Doors, Parliamentary Films, 1995

Order, Order, Britain's Parliament at Work, House of Commons, 1995

BOOKS

Sir Bryan Fell and K R Mackenzie, *The Houses of Parliament: A Guide to the Palace of Westminster*, HMSO, Fifteenth edition 1994

Stewart Ross, *The House of Commons*, Politics Today series, Wayland, 1986

Stewart Ross, *The House of Lords*, Politics Today series, Wayland, 1986

Robert Wilson, *The Houses of Parliament*, Jarrold, 1994

Picture acknowledgements
The publishers would like to thank the following for allowing their pictures to be reproduced: Ace Photo Agency: pages 21, 22, 25, 28-29, 30, 31 (top), 41; Bridgeman Art Library: pages 3, 9, 13, 44 (British Library), 11 (Stapleton Collection), 12 (O'Shea Gallery), 17, 27, 38 (Palace of Westminster), 34 (Towner Art Gallery); The British Library: page 7; Camera Press: pages 20, 33, 40; Mary Evans Picture Library: pages 23, 37; Illustrated London News: page 31 (bottom), 35; Jarrold Publishing: page 32; Reproduced by kind permission of the Palace of Westminster: pages 5, 10, 19, 26; Tony Stone Images: page 15; Topham Picturepoint: pages 15, 39, 42-43, 43; Wayland Picture Library: pages 8, 18, 36, 37 (bottom), 45; Zefa Pictures: front cover.

INDEX

Numbers in **bold** refer to illustrations.